PICTURE LIBRARY

SCUBA DIVING

SCUBA DIVING

Norman Barrett

Franklin Watts

London   New York   Sydney   Toronto

© 1988 Franklin Watts Ltd

First published in Great Britain
   1988 by
Franklin Watts Ltd
12a Golden Square
London W1R 4BA

First published in the USA by
Franklin Watts Inc
387 Park Avenue South
New York
NY 10016

First published in Australia by
Franklin Watts
14 Mars Road
Lane Cove
NSW 2066

UK ISBN: 0 86313 682 6
US ISBN: 0-531-10631-4
Library of Congress Catalog Card
Number 88-50372

Printed in Italy

Designed by
Barrett & Willard

Photographs by
Action Plus
John Evans/Action Plus
J. M. Twilley
N. S. Barrett Collection

Illustration by
Rhoda & Robert Burns

Technical Consultant
J. M. Twilley

Contents

Introduction

Scuba diving is an exciting underwater activity. Using special breathing apparatus, scuba divers explore the underwater world. It is a magical, fascinating world, peaceful, yet full of interest.

With modern equipment and methods, scuba diving is not a dangerous sport. But the strictest safety precautions should always be taken. Beginners must be supervised by instructors, and even experts should never dive alone.

△ A group of divers ready to go down. Although scuba equipment might look heavy and cumbersome, it is easy to manage once below the surface because of the buoyancy of the water.

People, unlike fish, need air to breathe. Scuba is a word made up from the initial letters of "Self-Contained Underwater Breathing Apparatus." The apparatus is a cylinder that contains compressed air and a "regulator" with which to breathe the air. This enables people to enjoy long periods underwater without coming up to breathe.

Scuba diving for recreation is called sport diving.

△ The scuba diver enjoys looking in on another world. The colorful animal and plant life in the water and on the sea floor is a never-ending source of pleasure for lovers of the sport.

The scuba diver

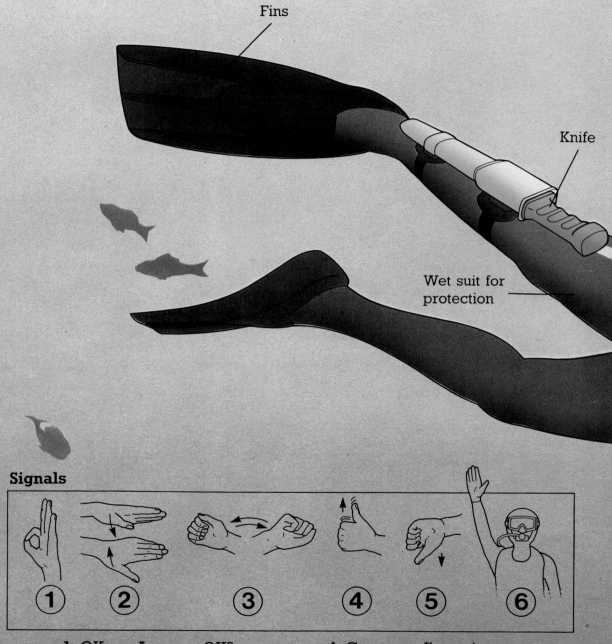

Fins

Knife

Wet suit for
protection

Signals

① ② ③ ④ ⑤ ⑥

1 OK, or Are you OK?
2 Something wrong.
3 Distress signal, emergency.

4 Go up, or I'm going up.
5 Go down, or I'm going down.
6 Stop, stay where you are.

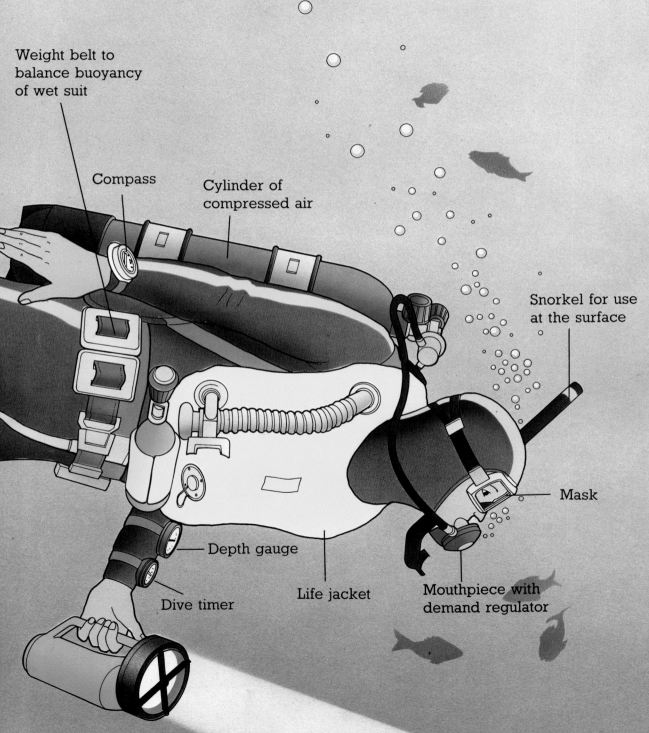

Weight belt to
balance buoyancy
of wet suit

Compass

Cylinder of
compressed air

Snorkel for use
at the surface

Mask

Depth gauge

Dive timer

Life jacket

Mouthpiece with
demand regulator

Diving dangers

Dangers of underwater sport include increased pressure at depth and the chance of something going wrong.

Special precautions have to be taken for deep diving, below about 10 m (33 ft). Divers must surface gradually to avoid "the bends," a serious sickness. Long dives must be carefully planned, so as not to run out of air. Diving with a companion, or "buddy," ensures there is help at hand in an emergency.

▷ Using a line from his boat, a diver makes a decompression stop. Divers use special tables which tell them how often they must stop and for how long, depending on the depth and duration of their dive.

▽ Buddy diving, or diving in pairs, is essential in case of emergency, such as running out of air or becoming entangled in a fishing line or with seaweed.

Diving for pleasure

The basics of underwater swimming may be learned in a swimming pool or shallow water, always with an instructor. Simple equipment, such as a snorkel, may be tried. Many people enjoy their first taste of underwater sports on vacation, snorkeling in warm waters.

Before taking up scuba diving, however, it is essential to undergo full training by an expert.

▽ Underwater swimming is largely a matter of confidence. Many people find it easier to swim underwater than on the surface. But you should never swim underwater or scuba dive if you have a cold or other illness.

Snorkeling is a pleasant pastime in itself and can be an exciting introduction to the underwater world. It is also useful in helping the diver to become accustomed to the underwater experience.

A snorkel is a device that allows a surface swimmer to breath without lifting his or her head out of the water. It is used with scuba equipment, too, to help the diver breathe while swimming on the surface.

△ A swimming pool is the best place to learn to snorkel, provided there is proper supervision. Snorkels have a mouthpiece you grip gently with your teeth. With the top of the tube above water, you breathe air through your mouth.

Scuba diving is not a "do-it-yourself" sport. The only way to learn is to take instruction. There is much to know about the use of equipment and about the dangers of diving and how to deal with them.

It is safer and more enjoyable to share the sport of underwater diving with others. Joining a scuba diving club is an excellent way to start the sport. You can also go to a diving school or take lessons on vacation.

▽ In warm, shallow waters, the delights of the underwater world may be enjoyed with just a snorkel. A mask helps the snorkeler to see more clearly underwater and fins help him or her move about more easily.

△ An instructor at the poolside explains how the demand regulator works.

◁ In some warm waters, scuba diving can be enjoyed without body protection. But there may be the danger of cuts from sharp coral, and, except in the warmest of waters, a long stay underwater produces chilling.

Good diving can be found all over
the world, and no one spot is quite
like another. You can dive in rivers
and from beaches, on coral islands in
the tropics, at night, in caves or even
under ice – all with proper training.

Much diving is done from boats.
This enables the diver to explore
deeper areas away from the shore.
For deep dives, a weighted line is
dropped from the boat, with markers
indicating decompression stops.

▽ Diving from boats has
many advantages. The
diving offshore is
usually deeper and the
visibility underwater
often better. It is also
easier to slip into the
sea from a boat than
from the shore, and
very little swimming has
to be done.

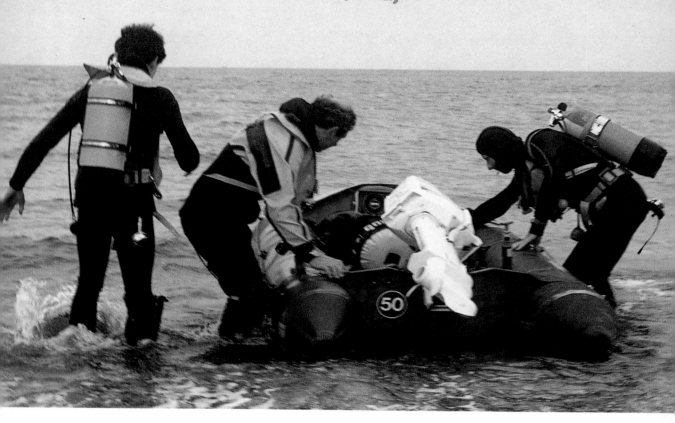

△ Inflatable rubber dinghies with outboard motors are a relatively cheap method of boat diving. The divers go to sea fully suited up, as there is no room to change in the boat. The boat should never be left unattended.

◁ One of the advantages of diving from a larger boat is that there is plenty of room for gear and equipment.

17

The underwater world

In many places, the underwater world is ablaze with color – tropical fish, other sea animals and plants. Yet without artificial light, very little color can be seen underwater, because the water filters out the sun's rays.

Even at a few feet down, much of the color is absorbed. The red is absorbed first, in about 5 m (16 ft), and most things look blue or green. Below about 25 m (80 ft), everything looks gray or black.

▷ A well-equipped diver swims down toward the sea floor in shallow water. The brightness above is from the sun.

▽ Without artificial light, everything a few feet down is blue or green.

▷ Artificial light turns
the sea floor into a
colorful landscape like
nothing seen above
ground. Shoals of
tropical fish swim
among the coral and
seaweed. Animals live
everywhere on the sea
bottom, from the shore
to the deepest parts of
the ocean. But plant life
may be found only as
deep as the sun's rays
reach.

The study of
underwater life is called
marine biology. Many
divers enjoy studying
marine life and use a
special underwater
slate for making notes.

△Things are not always what they
seem on the sea floor: a sea anemone
(top left), which looks like a flower but
is a sea animal, a fish (top right) that
looks like a sea anemone, and another
sea anemone (above).
◁A red fish and red coral.
▽Creatures that blend with their
surroundings: a fish (below left) and a
velvet swimming crab (below right).

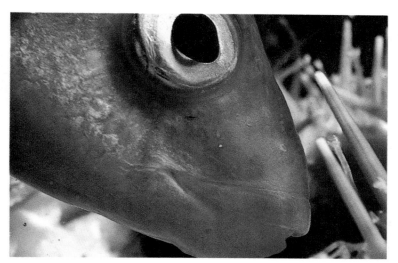

△ A clown fish, one fish that is safe in the stinging tentacles of the sea anemone. They protect it from other predators.

◁ A parrot fish, so called because of the shape of its beak.

▽ Beautifully colored tropical fish (below left) and a hermit crab (below).

Underwater photography

Amateur photographers can buy inexpensive cameras that have built-in flashes and are waterproof down to about 5 m (16 ft). Cameras made specially for underwater use give better results. Ordinary cameras with special watertight housings may be used. These are operated with large control knobs on the outside.

Floating particles of marine life or sand reduce visibility, but this is hardly noticeable in close-ups.

△ Often, the best way to photograph fish is to wait until something interesting swims past.

▷ An expert takes a close-up photograph with a camera and powerful flashgun steadied by support legs. Underwater cameras may have special devices to show what's in the picture, because the diving mask makes it impossible to put your eye close to a regular viewfinder.

Exploring wrecks

Deep wrecks must be investigated by divers with special equipment or remote controlled probes. But scuba divers with special training and equipment can explore the numerous wrecks of small ships.

Wrecks are of particular interest because of the collection of marine life attracted to them. Trophy hunters, on the other hand, are attracted by the promise of underwater treasure.

▽ The fish seem as curious as the diver examining part of a ship on the sea floor. Divers should never explore a wreck alone or without special training. Buddies should always be in visual contact, with perhaps another pair of divers outside as a saftey measure. A wet suit should be worn as protection against sharp projections and the cold. Divers also carry a knife in case they get caught in fishing nets or lines.

Underwater competition

Although scuba diving is an outdoor adventure sport, there are some underwater activities that can be classed as competitive sports.

Finswimming, racing with fins on, takes place in Olympic size pools.

Underwater orienteering involves accurate navigation of a specially designed underwater course.

Underwater hockey is played between teams.

△In underwater hockey, teams wear fins, masks and snorkels. They use a wooden stick and try to score goals by pushing a lead disc into their opponent's goal.

The story of scuba diving

The first divers

The first divers probably went underwater to collect shellfish for food, thousands of years ago. Then people dived for sponges or pearls. These divers could stay underwater only for as long as they could hold their breath.

Breathing underwater

To breathe underwater, a diver must take down his or her own supply of air. The first successful device for doing this was probably the diving bell. The ancient Greek philosopher and scientist Aristotle described a kind of diving bell over 2,000 years ago. It was a large container lowered upside-down

into the water with air trapped inside. The diver worked inside the bell until the oxygen in the air ran out.

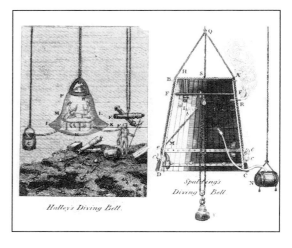

△ Old drawings of diving bells.

Improved diving bells

Diving bells were first so called when real bells were used, possibly a thousand years ago. The idea was improved and special containers were built. The first reliable record we have of a practical diving bell dates back to the early 1500s. It was designed by an Italian called Lorena.

The chief underwater interest in those days was in salvaging wrecks, often containing gold and other treasure. So there was a strong incentive to improve diving methods. One of the most successful diving bells was built

△ Lorena's diving bell looked nothing like a bell, but it worked on the same principle. The container is open to the water at the bottom, but the pressure of air inside it keeps the water out.

by the famous British astronomer Edmund Halley in 1690. He sent down barrels of fresh air to renew the supply. He also provided divers with individual "bells" which they wore on their heads. They breathed air through a tube linked with the main bell.

The diving helmet

Diving helmets were first used in the early 1800s, and became the

△ A cartoon of a diver in the early 1900s who had the "bad luck" to find a case of wine instead of the treasure he was looking for.

standard method for underwater exploration for nearly 150 years. The diver was lowered to the sea bottom in a watertight suit, weighed down with lead-soled boots. Air was pumped through a tube to the helmet, which had glass windows to look through. Advanced versions of the diving suit are still used today by commercial divers.

The aqualung

A number of improvements led to the development of the aqualung. The regulator, invented in 1865, controlled the amount of air the diver received. A compressed air cylinder that could withstand great pressure was developed in 1900, dispensing with the need for an airline. The aqualung, invented in 1943, was filled with compressed air, which the diver could breathe through a special valve, called a demand regulator, at the correct pressure.

The leading figure in the development of the aqualung was a French naval officer called Jacques Cousteau. It was largely through Cousteau's further research and his books and films that scuba diving became available to everyone and spread as a sport worldwide.

Facts and records

Pressure

The pressure of the air at sea level is 14·7 psi, or 1 atmosphere. This is due to the weight of the air in the atmosphere. Our bodies are not affected by this pressure, because we are born to it.

At a depth of 10 m (33 ft) underwater, the pressure is doubled to 2 atmospheres. At 20 m (66 ft) it is 3 atmospheres, and so on. As a diver goes down, any parts of the body or equipment that contain air, such as the lungs, are compressed. The aqualung's regulator supplies air to the diver at the same pressure as the surrounding water to compensate for this.

Deepest dive

The deepest recorded dive using scuba equipment was 133 m (437 ft) by two US divers, John Gruener and Neal Watson, in 1968. They recorded this depth off Freeport, in the Bahamas.

The first casualties

A Scotsman called Spalding and his son made improvements in Halley's diving bell before they died in one of their devices. They are thought to have suffocated, the first recorded casualties of diving.

△ A Spalding diving bell in use.

Glossary

Aqualung
Underwater breathing apparatus that includes the harness and demand regulator as well as the compressed air cylinder.

Bends
The common name given to decompression sickness. It is a condition caused by ascending too quickly from a deep dive. The nitrogen (a gas), which has dissolved into the blood and body tissues under extra pressure at depth appears as bubbles, with serious and sometimes fatal results.

Buddy
A diving companion. Buddy breathing is an emergency drill in which two or more divers share one aqualung using the same demand regulator.

Coral
A hard substance formed on the sea bottom by the skeletons of millions of tiny sea animals. Coral formations take all kinds of shapes and sizes.

Decompression
The lessening of pressure as a diver rises.

Demand regulator
A valve that adjusts the pressure of the compressed air in the cylinder to the pressure of the surrounding water, enabling the diver to breathe normally. The deeper a diver goes, the more compressed the air, so that the air supply is used more quickly at depth.

Diving bell
A device lowered into the water from which divers can work.

Marine biology
The science and study of underwater life.

Scuba
A word made up from the initial letters of "Self-Contained Underwater Breathing Apparatus."

Snorkel
A short tube with mouthpiece which enables the diver to breathe just under the surface of the water.

Wet suit
A scuba diving suit made of neoprene foam rubber that is not completely waterproof, but keeps the diver warm and provides protection.

Index